BRITISH
WARSHIPS
& AUXILIARIES

F94

THE ROYAL NAVY

"We can think of nothing more calculated to depress morale in the Royal Navy than failure to give an unqualified assurance that there will be no further cuts in RN capabilities in this Parliament."

House of Commons Defence Committee, October 1993

For the Royal Navy, 1993 was a year of grey skies, broken only by occasional glimpses of sunshine. And as it drew to a close, storm clouds were looming on the horizon as the Treasury once again targeted defence in its search for public spending economies. Any further cutbacks, coming just months after a series of major force reductions was announced, without a commensurate decrease in operational tasks, will place even larger question marks over the ability of the RN to fulfil current commitments. It is therefore all the more disturbing that Treasury leaks have sought to discredit the armed forces in the eyes of the public, portraying them as inefficient monoliths encumbered by top heavy commands.

Of course, continuing concerns over the size of the naval vote should not take the shine off the operational achievements of the past 12 months. In the Adriatic, the Royal Navy has maintained a permanent presence since the beginning of the year, supporting British forces ashore as part of Operation "Grapple", and enforcing embargoes against Serbia and Montenegro as part of a joint NATO/WEU force. Further afield, the nuclear submarine HMS TRIUMPH made a record breaking deployment to Australia via the Gulf, covering almost 47,000 miles (much of it submerged) in the process - all without base support.

Other achievements have taken a somewhat lower profile. Due to its sensitivity, the role which the RN has played in drug interdiction operations in the Caribbean has gained little publicity. Likewise in Hong Kong, where the interception of smugglers continues despite escalating violence against RN boarding parties. Both operations demonstrate the role which naval forces can (and do) play in support of civil powers.

The service has also had a major hand in peacekeeping and humanitarian aid operations. Sea King 4 helicopters of 845 Squadron, based at Split since November 1992, have been in the forefront of UN relief flights in former Yugoslavia. In Cambodia a 70-strong contingent of Royal Navy and Royal Marines personnel has served with the United Nations Naval Unit, patrolling the coastal waters and inland waterways as part of peacekeeping efforts.

The diversity of this very small cross-section of operational tasks is readily apparent, and increasingly typical of a very uncertain post-Cold War world. The threat of global war has recede into the distance, to be replaced by a greater emphasis on regional "bushfire" conflicts. This strategic shift means that the blue-water fleet of the Cold War era must now adjust to a new role. The change is more one of emphasis than of substance.

Defending Our Future?

The 1993 Statement on the Defence Estimates, Defending Our Future, was not the knockout punch to the RN which some had predicted.[1] Instead it left the service rocking on its heels - but still

2

in the ring! Significantly, the amphibious shipping replacement programme, the Navy Board's top priority, remained intact. Thus the concept of the balanced fleet - a mix of air capable ships, amphibious vessels, destroyers and frigates, submarines and mine countermeasures vessels - is still credible, although in places it must be stated "only just."

Defending Our Future broke new ground in its attempt to quantify military tasks and their allocated resources within three overlapping roles. As outlined, these were:

- Ensuring the protection and security of the UK and dependent territories.
- Insuring against any major external threat to the UK and allies
- Contributing to the UK's wider security interests through the maintenance of peace and international security.

Some 50 military tasks falling within these three roles were then detailed, along with the force levels considered necessary for each. Defence Secretary Malcolm Rifkind called it "...a framework to ensure we can maintain a balance between policy, commitments and resources".

How far it succeeded in that aim is debatable. The practice of "multiple earmarking" resources between the three defence roles makes the implicit assumption that some tasks will not be met simultaneously. The unexpected is simply not provided for.

Without doubt, the most controversial decision announced in Defending Our Future was that to withdraw from service the four virtually brand new Upholder class diesel-electric submarines. New hardware procured at a cost approaching £1 billion is to be sacrificed, bringing to an end conventional submarine operations in the Royal Navy. It left the service with a considerable amount of egg on its face, and comes as a great blow to all those who have been involved in the submarines introduction to service.

Nevertheless, the Navy Board has made its views quite clear. At a time when power projection has once again come to the fore, the mobility and endurance of the nuclear-powered attack submarine makes it a most powerful sea control asset. And, with a diminishing budget apparently unable to sustain both nuclear and conventional operations, the axe naturally fell on the latter. I n just one swipe of the axe a major part of "the teeth" were written off -with little indication of how the long promised cuts to the "tail" are to be made. It is still intended that the 12 Swiftsure and Trafalgar class SSNs should remain in service, the former being replaced by a new Batch 2 Trafalgar early in the next century.

In hindsight, the very characteristics of the Upholder design perhaps contributed to its downfall. Its size and sophistication approached that of an SSN, but speed and endurance betrayed the limitations of conventional diesel-electric propulsion. With a projected air independent propulsion system still a decade away, the gap in performance weighed heavily in favour of the SSN. This despite the huge running costs of an SSN which were made public during 1993 (Swiftsure Class £19.5 m: Trafalgar Class £10.5m and Upholder Class £2m-per year)

Of course, with the withdrawal of the SSK the service will be discarding capabilities which nuclear-powered boats cannot fully emulate. Special forces insertion in shallow water is the prime case, a role which the now retired Oberon class performed with distinction in both the Falklands and the Gulf. Naval sources confirm that SSNs will now take on special forces operations, although their operating envelope will obviously be more constrained.

The SSK will also be sorely missed in training. The RN -and RAF Nimrod force will in future have to "hire" a submarine from elsewhere in NATO to participate in exercise scenarios. (Spain and The Netherlands have already provided submarines for exercises) Likewise, ASW helicopter training is already suffering from a lack of sub-surface assets.

While the withdrawal of the Upholders grabbed the headlines, the Royal Navy's surface fleet was also hard hit. Numbers of destroyers and frigates fell from the NOW famous "about 40" (in fact 38) mark to the equally vague "about 35" figure, reflecting the paying off of the elderly Type 21 and

3

Leander class frigates and the slowness in ordering further Type 23s.

With no decrease in the number of national and NATO directed tasks the fleet's "workhorses" are now being stretched to unprecedented levels. It was indeed strange to be at sea during the year in one of HM ships with 50% of the Ships company on leave. A form of "flexible rostering" is likely to be introduced in 1994 to alleviate some of the strain, allowing ships to remain at extended notice for some tasks. But programming will remain very taut with little margin for operational contingencies.

Mine countermeasures (MCM), as so often in the past, is also being neglected. Yet the mine, now as much as ever before, still represents the most cost-effective means of sea denial- especially to any island nation. Moreover, its low cost and abundant supply may increasingly endear it to terrorist groups -or foreign power. In spite of this threat, the MCM flotilla is continuing to contract. The goal of 40 mine countermeasures vessels (MCMVs) set in 1990 was first whittled down to 34, and latterly to just 25. But with the withdrawal in 1993 of the last of the obsolete "Ton" class MCMVs, and the paying off or re-assignment of the operationally limited "River" class minesweepers, the Royal Navy will be left with 13 "Hunt" class dual-role MCMVs and 5 "Sandown" class, a mere 18 ships in all. Orders for more Sandowns have been consistently delayed.

In a detailed report released in October 1993 naval analyst Eric Grove warned: "The mine threat is of particular importance for the United Kingdom which is surrounded by shallow waters subject to mining, which relies on a sea-based nuclear deterrent and which has interests in the free passage of shipping in other areas where mines could be a threat."[2] He concluded: "It is risky enough having only 18 assets to cope with near term uncertainties; reducing still further Britain's ability to cope with the incalculable risks of the next century seems most ill advised."

Without doubt the greatest encouragement for the service was the order for the Landing Platform Helicopter (LPH) HMS OCEAN. But the Navy had to fight hard to retain the ship in its forward programme. Central Staff recommendations to cancel the LPH procurement were only reversed after Ministers had seen the appaling conditions which troops had to endure on board RFA ARGUS, the ad hoc LPH deployed to the Adriatic early in the year.

The ramifications of the LPH procurement were considerable. Swan Hunter, which had expected to win the contract, fell into receivership when a substantially lower bid from VSEL triumphed. But, more importantly, the decision to proceed with LPH fully endorsed Navy Board policy priorities and reaffirmed the Government's commitment to an effective amphibious capability: a judgement against might well have undermined plans for the replacement of the ageing Landing Platform Dock (LPD) vessels FEARLESS and INTREPID.

In the event, the two LPD replacements remain a key part of the RN/RM long term force structure. Nevertheless, the protracted nature of the project definition phase, which has required substantial revision to meet revised "cost-capped" targets, has served to delay the procurement process. One area being studied is the feasibility of introducing commercial standards into areas of the LPD design without compromising traditional warship safety and integrity.

Given these delays, a contract for the first vessel is now unlikely before late 1995 at the earliest. In the meantime FEARLESS soldiers on, her running costs spiralling and her material condition worsening.

Another area to have escaped cuts is the RN's carrier force. INVINCIBLE and ARK ROYAL are currently operational with ILLUSTRIOUS due to re-emerge from major refit during 1994. The Sea Harrier FRS.2, most significant advance in naval aviation in over a decade, will also enter service during the coming year. With the latest Blue Vixen radar and AIM-120 AMRAAM air-to-air missile, the FRS.2 will be a most formidable maritime interceptor.

Progress on the new strategic nuclear deterrent force continues apace. The first deterrent patrol with the Trident D5 system is expected to commence in late 1994/early 1995. HMS VANGUARD, first of a class of four new "bombers", was commissioned in August and signed over to the RN a month later. Her sister VICTORIOUS was rolled out in September '93 and will begin sea trials in 1994.

At a total cost of around £10 billion, there is little doubt that Britain has bought itself a "gold plated" deterrent solution. When the decision to buy was made in 1981, Trident was probably the only credible choice to penetrate the anticipated Soviet anti-ballistic missile defences. Now it looks like overkill, with the designed complement of 128 warheads per boat unlikely to ever be deployed. Thus, given the latent capacity in the system, it is only sensible that a single-warhead Trident system should assume the sub-strategic nuclear role when the Royal Air Force retire its WE177 free-fall bomb early in the next century. Although an air-launched weapon may have marginally greater tactical flexibility, its £2 billion price tag was unjustifiable in today's budgetary climate.

But even with this subsidiary mission, the Trident patrol will continue to be a drain on the navy's budget and it is therefore imperative that operating economies are considered. Dual-crewing the SSBNs with Port and Starboard complements is one costly anachronism which cries out for reform. Some form of rotational manning would be far more cost effective. And, given the far greater range and accuracy of Trident, every option to reduce the cost of the current operational cycle should be examined. The caveat remains, of course, that one boat must remain fully operational on patrol at all times.

Reserved Judgement

One of the most contentious issues in the past year has been the restructuring of the reserve forces. Despite advertisements for new recruits in the press a few weeks previous, proposals were announced in June '93 in which the Royal Naval Reserve (RNR) lost its deep water minesweeping role, had 11 of its 24 shore centres earmarked for closure and saw its numbers cut by 1,200 people. In addition, the 2,700-strong Royal Naval Auxiliary Service (RNXS), found itself without a role and will disband in March 1994.

For the RNR, the loss of the 10th Mine Countermeasures Squadron had long been expected, the deep water mine threat having largely disappeared with the end of the Cold War. A sea-going branch will offer some reservists the chance to serve with the front-line navy, but integration is likely to prove difficult. Moreover, it will have only limited practical appeal to most "week-end" sailors. A move towards an RNR mainly of ex RN regulars seems more likely than todays force of civilian part timers. The decision has greatly upset the RNR who until now have kept the White Ensign flying away from the traditional naval areas of the UK.

Similarly, there is no point in denying that the traditional roles of the RNXS, namely naval control of shipping and the defence of ports and anchorages, have diminished. But there are other tasks for which both it and the RNR are ideally suited, including search and rescue, maritime disaster support, counter-terrorist duties, HM Coast Guard and Customs and Excise support. However, the restructuring proposals, driven by budget cuts, made no attempt to reflect these opportunities and roles. The result, sadly, is a naval reserve with reduced appeal and less relevance to the public from which it draws its all important support.

Fleet Support Cuts - More Pain, Little Gain

Much has been said in recent years regarding cutting the "tail" to match the "teeth". A smaller, more efficient front-line clearly needs less support and there is undoubtedly wide scope for rationalisation. Unfortunately, many of the potential savings have been sacrificed at the political altar.

The last two years have seen a major review of the future role of the Royal Dockyards, capped by the at times farcical bidding process for nuclear submarine (including Trident) refits. The credibility of the costings prepared by management contractors at Rosyth and Devonport remains in doubt, but the Navy Board had its way and selected Devonport as its sole nuclear facility.

It is a well known fact that Devonport, together with other private shipbuilders and ship repair yards, are quite capable of handling the entire refit and repair workload for all the submarine and surface ships in the Fleet. But politics prevented the closure of Rosyth Royal Dockyard (as they had done with the adjacent naval base two years before) leaving the RN's surface ship refit programme wedded to the yard for the next decade. There is no great enthusiasm to retain the facilities within the RN or Treasury. Whether there is room for both Dockyards after privatisation remains to be seen - it appears that by putting the facilities in commercial hands, the Government is finally looking to absolve itself of any future socio-economic responsibilities when the Rosyth yard is, inevitably, closed.

Another highly controversial announcement in 1993 was the decision to close down Portland Naval Base, home of Flag Officer Sea Training. Instead, sea training will move to a new base at Devonport though, once again, comparative investment appraisals are not totally convincing. An imaginative alternative - the use of a forward repair/depot ship as a mobile facility - was regrettably dropped at an early stage.

One trend which will continue is the contractorisation of second-line duties, with further opportunities arising from the Government's many "market testing" initiatives. For the navy this is nothing new - it first "civilianisation" dates back to the time of Henry VIII, and third and fourth line support has traditionally been performed by civilian labour. Nevertheless, there is a duty to keep a close watch on the ratio of uniformed and civilian personnel and the ability to regenerate forces at short notice.

Staying Afloat?

Does anyone care - or even notice - that the size of this island nation's once great Navy (and just as important) Merchant Marine have been whittled away year after year? For the RN It is regretfully true that it is very much a case of "out of sight - out of mind" for most of our peoples. In the current financial climate it appears to be very much a case of "He who shouts loudest...." is heard when it is time to share out the available funds. There are highly professional and vocal loby organisations at work today - there is certainly a job for them to do on behalf of the Navy. Unfortunately "the rules" forbid the Navy mounting a proper co-ordinated lobbying exercise.

There is no doubt that our political leaders take a lot of interest in their personal mailbags - especially those in marginal constituencies. There have been some remarkable incidents during 1993 of "ordinary members of the public" alerting their MP's over items concerning them regarding the defence of this country. It would be good to think that the headlines thus generated must eventually bear some fruit particularly at this critical time when the patent mismatch of commitments and allocated resources is now stretching the Royal Navy to the extreme.

1   Defending Our Future - Statement on the Defence Estimates 1993. Cm 2270. HMSO
2   Eric Grove, The Sandown Gap - The United Kingdom's Requirement for Minehunters. Prepared for Vosper Thornycroft (UK) Ltd, October 1993

SHIPS OF THE ROYAL NAVY
Pennant Numbers

Ship	Pennant Number	Ship	Pennant Number
Aircraft Carriers		BOXER	F92
		BEAVER	F93
INVINCIBLE	R05	BRAVE	F94
ILLUSTRIOUS •	R06	LONDON	F95
ARK ROYAL	R07	SHEFFIELD	F96
		COVENTRY	F98
Destroyers		CORNWALL	F99
		ACTIVE	F171
BIRMINGHAM	D86	ARROW	F173
NEWCASTLE	D87	ALACRITY	F174
GLASGOW	D88	AVENGER	F185
EXETER	D89	LANCASTER	F229
SOUTHAMPTON	D90	NORFOLK	F230
NOTTINGHAM	D91	ARGYLL	F231
LIVERPOOL	D92	MARLBOROUGH	F233
MANCHESTER	D95	IRON DUKE	F234
GLOUCESTER	D96	MONMOUTH	F235
EDINBURGH	D97	MONTROSE	F236
YORK	D98	WESTMINSTER	F237
CARDIFF	D108	NORTHUMBERLAND	F238
		RICHMOND	F239
Frigates		SOMERSET	F240
		GRAFTON	F241
ANDROMEDA •	F57	SUTHERLAND	F242
CUMBERLAND	F85		
CAMPBELTOWN	F86	**Submarines**	
CHATHAM	F87		
BROADSWORD	F88	RESOLUTION	S22
BATTLEAXE	F89	REPULSE	S23
BRILLIANT	F90	RENOWN	S26
BRAZEN	F91	VANGUARD	S28

Ship	Pennant Number	Ship	Pennant Number
UPHOLDER	S40	BICESTER	M36
UNSEEN	S41	CHIDDINGFOLD	M37
URSULA	S42	ATHERSTONE	M38
UNICORN	S43	HURWORTH	M39
TRENCHANT	S91	BERKELEY	M40
TALENT	S92	QUORN	M41
TRIUMPH	S93	SANDOWN	M101
VALIANT	S102	INVERNESS	M102
SCEPTRE	S104	CROMER	M103
SPARTAN	S105	WALNEY	M104
SPLENDID	S106	BRIDPORT	M105
TRAFALGAR	S107	WILTON	M1116
SOVEREIGN	S108	WAVENEY ●	M2003
SUPERB	S109	CARRON ●	M2004
TURBULENT	S110	DOVEY ●	M2005
TIRELESS	S117	HELFORD ●	M2006
TORBAY	S118	HUMBER	M2007
		BLACKWATER	M2008

Assault Ships

Ship	Pennant Number	Ship	Pennant Number
		ITCHEN	M2009
		HELMSDALE ●	M2010
FEARLESS	L10	ORWELL	M2011
INTREPID ●	L11	RIBBLE ●	M2012
		SPEY	M2013
		ARUN	M2014

Minesweepers & Minehunters

Patrol Craft

Ship	Pennant Number	Ship	Pennant Number
BRECON	M29		
LEDBURY	M30	PEACOCK	P239
CATTISTOCK	M31	PLOVER	P240
COTTESMORE	M32	STARLING	P241
BROCKLESBY	M33	LEEDS CASTLE	P258
MIDDLETON	M34	REDPOLE	P259
DULVERTON	M35	KINGFISHER	P260

Ship	Pennant Number	Ship	Pennant Number
CYGNET	P261	**Survey Ships & RN**	
ARCHER	P264	**Manned Auxiliaries**	
DUMBARTON CASTLE	P265		
BITER	P270	BRITANNIA	A00
SMITER	P272	GLEANER	A86
PURSUER	P273	MESSINA	A107
ANGLESEY	P277	ROEBUCK	A130
ALDERNEY	P278	HECLA	A133
BLAZER	P279	HERALD	A138
DASHER	P280	ENDURANCE	A171
PUNCHER	P291	IRONBRIDGE	A311
CHARGER	P292	BULLDOG	A317
RANGER	P293	IXWORTH	A318
TRUMPETER	P294	BEAGLE	A319
GUERNSEY	P297		
SHETLAND	P298		
ORKNEY	P299		
LINDISFARNE	P300	• *Ships in reserve/long refit*	

This book is updated and re-issued every *December*. Keep up to date … Don't miss the new edition.

Phone 0579 343663 for details.

HMS Vanguard

VANGUARD CLASS

Ship	Pennant Number	Completion Date	Builder
VANGUARD	S28	1992	Vickers
VICTORIOUS		1994	Vickers
VIGILANT			Vickers

Displacement 15,000 tons (dived) **Dimensions** 150m x 13m x 12m **Speed** 25 + dived **Armament** 16 - Lockheed Trident 2 (D5) missiles, 4 Torpedo Tubes **Complement** 135 (Two crews).

Notes
VANGUARD sailed from her builders at Barrow in October 1992 for initial sea trials. A fourth vessel has been ordered and will probably be named VALIANT in due course.

HMS Renown

RESOLUTION CLASS

Ship	Pennant Number	Completion Date	Builder
RESOLUTION	S22	1967	Vickers
REPULSE	S23	1968	Vickers
RENOWN	S26	1968	C. Laird

Displacement 8,400 tons (submerged) **Dimensions** 130m x 10m x 9m **Speed** 25 knots **Armament** 16 Polaris missiles, 6 Torpedo Tubes **Complement** 147 (Two crews).

Notes

These three nuclear-powered Polaris submarines have been the United Kingdom's contribution to NATO's strategic nuclear deterrent since the late 1960's. Despite their age one of these submarines has been kept constantly on patrol. Thanks to their high speed, long endurance underwater, and advanced sonar and electronic equipment they have little fear of detection.

Each submarine carries 16 Polaris two-stage ballistic missiles, powered by solid fuel rocket motors, 9.45 metres long, 1.37 metres diameter and weighting 12,700 kilogrammes with a range of 2,500 miles. REVENGE paid off 1992. The 3 remaining vessels of the Class will gradually leave the Fleet as the Vanguard Class come into service.

SUBMARINES

HMS Valiant

VALIANT CLASS

Ship	Pennant Number	Completion Date	Builder
VALIANT	S102	1966	Vickers

Displacement 4,900 tons (dived) **Dimensions** 87m x 10m x 8m **Speed** 28 knots + **Armament** 6 Torpedo Tubes **Complement** 103.

Notes
The "last of the first" truly British nuclear powered submarines in service. VALIANT spent little time operational during 1993 and is expected to be declared surplus to requirements shortly. CHURCHILL and DREADNOUGHT – the forerunners of this class -are awaiting disposal at Rosyth with CONQUEROR, COURAGEOUS and WARSPITE at Devonport. . Discussions continue regarding the safe disposal of these vessels but no solution seems imminent.

● HMS NEPTUNE

HMS Sceptre

SWIFTSURE CLASS

Ship	Pennant Number	Completion Date	Builder
SCEPTRE	S104	1978	Vickers
SPARTAN	S105	1979	Vickers
SPLENDID	S106	1980	Vickers
SOVEREIGN	S108	1974	Vickers
SUPERB	S109	1976	Vickers

Displacement 4,500 tons dived **Dimensions** 83m x 10m x 8m **Speed** 30 knots + dived **Armament** 5 Torpedo Tubes **Complement** 116.

Notes

A follow-on class of ships from the Valiant Class. The Class are now based at Faslane. SWIFTSURE is awaiting disposal at Rosyth and could be joined by others of the class if further economies have to be made.

HMS Turbulent

TRAFALGAR CLASS

Ship	Pennant Number	Completion Date	Builder
TRENCHANT	S91	1989	Vickers
TALENT	S92	1990	Vickers
TRIUMPH	S93	1991	Vickers
TRAFALGAR	S107	1983	Vickers
TURBULENT	S110	1984	Vickers
TIRELESS	S117	1985	Vickers
TORBAY	S118	1986	Vickers

Displacement 4,500 tons **Dimensions** 85m x 10m x 8m **Speed** 30 + dived **Armament** 5 Torpedo Tubes **Complement** 125.

Notes
Enhanced development of the Swiftsure Class. Quieter, faster and with greater endurance than their predecessors. Design option studies into a new Batch 2 Trafalgar Class have been completed. Orders are expected to be placed in the mid to late 90's- but could become a victim of any further defence cuts.

HMS Unicorn

UPHOLDER CLASS

Ship	Pennant Number	Completion Date	Builder
UPHOLDER	S40	1989	Vickers
UNSEEN	S41	1991	Cammell Laird
URSULA	S42	1992	Cammell Laird
UNICORN	S43	1993	Cammell Laird

Displacement 2,400 tons (dived) **Dimensions** 70m x 8m x 5m **Speed** 20 knots dived **Armament** 6 Torpedo Tubes: Sub Harpoon missile **Complement** 44.

Notes

A new class of conventionally powered submarines. Of 19 proposed vessels only the ships listed above have been built. As a result of Defence economies announced in 1993 all the class are being offered for sale/ lease overseas. They will pay off during 1994/5.

• MARITIME PHOTOGRAPHIC

HMS Invincible

INVINCIBLE CLASS

Ship	Pennant Number	Completion Date	Builder
INVINCIBLE	R05	1979	Vickers
ILLUSTRIOUS	R06	1982	Swan Hunter
ARK ROYAL	R07	1985	Swan Hunter

Displacement 19,500 tons **Dimensions** 206m x 32m x 6.5m **Speed** 28 knots **Armament** Sea Dart Missile, 2 - 20mm guns, 3 Phalanx/Goalkeeper **Aircraft** 8 - Sea Harrier, 12 - Sea King **Complement** 900 + aircrews.

Notes

Manpower problems dictate that two ships are kept in the operational fleet, with the third in refit or reserve. ILLUSTRIOUS is expected to complete a lengthy refit at Devonport at the end of 1994. ARK ROYAL will then reduce to reserve/refit status.

16

HMS Fearless

FEARLESS CLASS

Ship	Pennant Number	Completion Date	Builder
FEARLESS	L10	1965	Harland & Wolff
INTREPID	L11	1967	J. Brown

Displacement 12,500 tons, 19,500 tons (flooded) **Dimensions** 158m x 24m x 8m **Speed** 20 knots **Armament** 2 Sea Cat Missile Systems, 2 - 40mm guns, 4 - 30mm + 2 - 20mm (INTREPID only) 2 - Vulcan Phalanx (FEARLESS only) **Complement** 580.

Notes

Multi-purpose ships that can operate helicopters for embarked Royal Marine Commandos. 4 landing craft are carried on an internal deck and are flooded out when the ship docks down. INTREPID paid off in 1991. A decision was made in late 1991 that both vessels would be replaced but financial restraints have delayed any order being made. As a result of their age both ships have become extremely expensive to keep operational..Limited refitting work underway (during 1993)onboard INTREPID as she may be required for further sea service if no new order for replacements materialise.

17

ASSAULT SHIPS

HMS Southampton

SHEFFIELD CLASS
(Type 42) Batch 1 & 2

Ship	Pennant Number	Completion Date	Builder
BIRMINGHAM	D86	1976	C. Laird
NEWCASTLE	D87	1978	Swan Hunter
GLASGOW	D88	1978	Swan Hunter
EXETER	D89	1980	Swan Hunter
SOUTHAMPTON	D90	1981	Vosper T.
NOTTINGHAM	D91	1982	Vosper T.
LIVERPOOL	D92	1982	C. Laird
CARDIFF	D108	1979	Vickers

Displacement 3,660 tons **Dimensions** 125m x 15m x 7m **Speed** 29 knots **Armament** 1 - 4.5" gun, 4 - 20mm guns, Sea Dart Missile System: 2 - Phalanx, Lynx Helicopter, 6 Torpedo Tubes **Complement** 280 +.

Notes
Sister Ships SHEFFIELD and COVENTRY lost in 1982 during the Falklands conflict. All ships have been modernised with new radar and electronic warfare systems.

● OFFICIAL PHOTO

HMS Manchester

SHEFFIELD CLASS
(Type 42) Batch 3

Ship	Pennant Number	Completion Date	Builder
MANCHESTER	D95	1983	Vickers
GLOUCESTER	D96	1984	Vosper T.
EDINBURGH	D97	1985	C. Laird
YORK	D98	1984	Swan Hunter

Displacement 4,775 tons **Dimensions** 132m x 15m x 7m **Speed** 30 knots + **Armament** 1- 4.5" gun, 1- Phalanx, 4 - 20mm guns. Sea Dart missile system. Lynx Helicopter, 6 Torpedo Tubes **Complement** 301.

Notes
"Stretched' versions of earlier ships of this class. Designed to provide area defence of a task force. Deck edge stiffening fitted to counter increased hull stress. EDINBURGH emerged from refit in late 1990 with new bow and forward mounted Phalanx. Studies continue(with France & Italy)) on the requirement for a Common New Generation Frigate.

19

D
E
S
T
R
O
Y
E
R
S

HMS Brazen

BROADSWORD CLASS
(Type 22) Batch 1

Ship	Pennant Number	Completion Date	Builder
BROADSWORD	F88	1978	Yarrow
BATTLEAXE	F89	1980	Yarrow
BRILLIANT	F90	1981	Yarrow
BRAZEN	F91	1982	Yarrow

Displacement 3,860 tons **Dimensions** 131m x 15m x 6m **Speed** 29 knots **Armament** 4 Exocet Missiles, 2 Sea Wolf Missile Systems, 4 - 30mm guns, 2 or 4 - 20mm guns, 6 Torpedo Tubes, 2 Lynx Helicopters **Complement** 224.

Notes
Successor to the successful Leander Class. Although capable of carrying 2 helicopters, only 1 normally embarked. These ships have been refitted with additional accommodation and classroom facilities and deploy as Initial Sea Training ships in a rota of two ships as a time.

HMS Beaver

BROADSWORD CLASS
(Type 22) Batch 2

Ship	Pennant Number	Completion Date	Builder
BOXER	F92	1983	Yarrow
BEAVER	F93	1984	Yarrow
BRAVE•	F94	1985	Yarrow
LONDON •	F95	1986	Yarrow
SHEFFIELD •	F96	1987	Swan Hunter
COVENTRY •	F98	1988	Swan Hunter

Displacement 4100 tons **Dimensions** 143m x 15m x 6m **Speed** 30 knots **Armament** 4 Exocet Missiles, 2 Sea Wolf Missile Systems, 4 - 30mm + 2 - 20mm guns, 6 Torpedo Tubes, 2 Lynx Helicopters **Complement** 273.

Notes
• Ships have enlarged hangar and flight deck. A Sea King can be, and is, carried in some ships of this class.All ships have an intelligence gathering capability.

21

FRIGATES

HMS Cumberland

BROADSWORD CLASS
(Type 22) Batch 3

Ship	Pennant Number	Completion Date	Builder
CUMBERLAND	F85	1988	Yarrow
CAMPBELTOWN	F86	1988	C. Laird
CHATHAM	F87	1989	Swan Hunter
CORNWALL	F99	1987	Yarrow

Displacement 4,200 tons **Dimensions** 147m x 15m x 7m **Speed** 30 knots **Armament** 1 - 4.5" gun, 1 - Goalkeeper, 8- Harpoon, 2- Seawolf, 4 - 30mm guns, 6 Torpedo Tubes, 2 Lynx or 1 Sea King Helicopter **Complement** 250.

Notes
General purpose gun and Goalkeeper system added to these ships as a direct result of lessons learned during Falklands conflict. All these ships have a major A/S and intelligence gathering capability. Cost £180 million each.

22

● MARITIME PHOTOGRAPHIC

HMS Monmouth

DUKE CLASS (Type 23)

Ship	Pennant Number	Completion Date	Builder
LANCASTER	F229	1991	Yarrow
NORFOLK	F230	1989	Yarrow
ARGYLL	F231	1991	Yarrow
MARLBOROUGH	F233	1991	Swan Hunter
IRON DUKE	F234	1992	Yarrow
MONMOUTH	F235	1993	Yarrow
MONTROSE	F236	1993	Yarrow
WESTMINSTER	F237	1993	Swan Hunter
NORTHUMBERLAND	F238	1994	Swan Hunter
RICHMOND	F239	1994	Swan Hunter

Displacement 3,500 tons **Dimensions** 133m x 15m x 5m **Speed** 28 knots **Armament** Harpoon & Seawolf missile systems: 1 - 4.5" gun, 4 - 2 twin, magazine launched, Torpedo Tubes **Complement** 157.

Notes
Three further ships, SOMERSET (F240), GRAFTON (F241) and SUTHERLAND (F242) ordered during 1991. Due for completion in 1995/7.

HMS Andromeda

LEANDER CLASS

Ship	Pennant Number	Completion Date	Builder
ANDROMEDA	F57	1968	HM Dockyard Portsmouth

Displacement 2,962 tons **Dimensions** 113m x 13m x 5m **Speed** 27 knots **Armament** Sea Wolf System, 4 - Exocet Missiles, 2 - 20mm guns, 6Torpedo Tubes, 1 Lynx helicopter **Complement** 260.

Notes

Having served the Fleet extremely well over 25 years the last of the Leander Class finally left the active Fleet at the end of 1993 when SCYLLA paid off for disposal. After a lengthy Rosyth refit ANDROMEDA was placed in extended reserve at Portsmouth during 1993.

HMS Active

AMAZON CLASS
(Type 21)

Ship	Pennant Number	Completion Date	Builder
ACTIVE	F171	1977	Vosper T.
ARROW	F173	1976	Yarrow
ALACRITY	F174	1977	Yarrow
AVENGER	F185	1978	Yarrow

Displacement 3,250 tons **Dimensions** 117m x 13m x 6m **Speed** 30 knots **Armament** 1 - 4.5" gun, 2- 20mm guns, 4 Exocet Missiles, 1 Sea Cat Missile System, 1 Lynx helicopter, 6 Torpedo Tubes **Complement** 170.

Notes
Sister ships ANTELOPE and ARDENT lost during the Falklands conflict. All 4 ships have been given extra hull strengthening. This class (built to a commercial design, and subsequently sold to the Ministry of Defence) have received no major mid-life modernisation. AMAZON & AMBUSCADE sold to Pakistan in 1993.The remainder of the class will follow during 1994.

● OFFICIAL PHOTO

HMS Bicester

MINE COUNTERMEASURES SHIPS (MCMV'S) BRECON CLASS

Ship	Pennant Number	Completion Date	Builder
BRECON	M29	1980	Vosper T.
LEDBURY	M30	1981	Vosper T.
CATTISTOCK	M31	1982	Vosper T.
COTTESMORE	M32	1983	Yarrow
BROCKLESBY	M33	1983	Vosper T.
MIDDLETON	M34	1984	Yarrow
DULVERTON	M35	1983	Vosper T.
BICESTER	M36	1986	Vosper T.
CHIDDINGFOLD	M37	1984	Vosper T.
ATHERSTONE	M38	1987	Vosper T.
HURWORTH	M39	1985	Vosper T.
BERKELEY	M40	1988	Vosper T.
QUORN	M41	1989	Vosper T.

Displacement 625 tonnes **Dimensions** 60m x 10m x 2.2m **Speed** 17 knots **Armament** 1x30mm + 2 x 20mm guns **Complement** 45.

Notes

The largest warships ever built of glass reinforced plastic. Designed to replace the Coniston Class – their cost (£35m each) has dictated the size of the class. Very sophisticated ships – and lively seaboats! During 1992 some vessels were used in a Fishery Protection role.

● OFFICIAL PHOTO

HMS Blackwater

FLEET MINESWEEPERS
RIVER CLASS

Ship	Pennant Number	Completion Date	Builder
WAVENEY ●	M2003	1984	Richards
CARRON ●	M2004	1984	Richards
DOVEY ●	M2005	1984	Richards
HELFORD ●	M2006	1984	Richards
HUMBER	M2007	1985	Richards
BLACKWATER +	M2008	1985	Richards
ITCHEN +	M2009	1985	Richards
HELMSDALE	M2010	1985	Richards
ORWELL	M2011	1985	Richards
RIBBLE	M2012	1985	Richards
SPEY +	M2013	1985	Richards
ARUN +	M2014	1986	Richards

Displacement 850 tonnes **Dimensions** 47m x 10m x 3m **Speed** 14 knots **Armament** 1- 40mm + 2- GPMG **Complement** 30.

Notes
MCM ships built for service with the RNR.All are to be withdrawn however during 1994 as a result of 1993 defence economies. BLACKWATER has been in the FIshery Protection Squadron (FPS) with an RN crew. HELMSDALE and RIBBLE laid up (at Portsmouth) in 1991 as a defence economy and those marked ● followed in 1993. Those marked + are expected to re-deploy to the Northern Ireland Squadron and ORWELL to BRNC Dartmouth (Vice WILTON)in late 1994. The Remainder will be sold.

● D. HANNAFORD

HMS Wilton

TON CLASS

Ship	Pennant Number	Completion Date	Builder
WILTON	M1116	1973	Vosper T.

Displacement 425 tons **Dimensions** 46m x 9m x 3m **Speed** 15 knots **Armament** 1 - 40mm gun **Complement** 29.

Notes

120 of this class were built in the early 50s -all of the original class have now been sold overseas or scrapped. They fulfilled many roles over the years and gave excellent service. WILTON, built of glassfibre, was the world's first 'plastic' warship. She is a training ship for BRNC Dartmouth but will be replaced by ORWELL in 1994. SOBERTON paid off in 1992 for a static role with the Sea Cadet Corps at Erith. IVESTON is in use by the Sea Cadets at Thurrock and KELLINGTON has a similar role at Stockton on Tees.

HMS Bridport

SANDOWN CLASS

Ship	Pennant Number	Completion Date	Builder
SANDOWN	M101	1989	Vosper T.
INVERNESS	M102	1991	Vosper T.
CROMER	M103	1991	Vosper T.
WALNEY	M104	1992	Vosper T.
BRIDPORT	M105	1993	Vosper T.

Displacement 450 tons **Dimensions** 53m x 10m x 2m **Speed** 13 knots **Armament** 1 - 30mm gun **Complement** 34.

Notes

A new class dedicated to a single mine hunting role. Propulsion is by vectored thrust and bow thrusters. Up to 15 more ships were planned, but the 7 due to be ordered in 1991 were postponed. Six similar ships are being built for Saudi Arabia.

● OFFICIAL PHOTO

HMS Leeds Castle

CASTLE CLASS

Ship	Pennant Number	Completion Date	Builder
LEEDS CASTLE	P258	1981	Hall Russell
DUMBARTON CASTLE	P265	1982	Hall Russell

Displacement 1,450 tons **Dimensions** 81m x 11m x 3m **Speed** 20 knots **Armament** 1 - 40mm gun **Complement** 40.

Notes

These ships have a dual role – that of fishery protection and offshore patrols within the limits of UK territorial waters. Unlike the Island Class these ships are able to operate helicopters – including Sea King aircraft. Trials have been conducted to assess the suitability of these ships as Minelayers. DUMBARTON CASTLE is currently on long term deployment to the Falkland Islands with her ships' company rotating every four months.

HMS Lindisfarne

ISLAND CLASS

Ship	Pennant Number	Completion Date	Builder
ANGLESEY	P277	1979	Hall Russell
ALDERNEY	P278	1979	Hall Russell
GUERNSEY	P297	1977	Hall Russell
SHETLAND	P298	1977	Hall Russell
ORKNEY	P299	1977	Hall Russell
LINDISFARNE	P300	1978	Hall Russell

Displacement 1,250 tons **Dimensions** 60m x 11m x 4m **Speed** 17 knots **Armament** 1 - 40mm gun **Complement** 39.

Notes

Built on trawler lines these ships were introduced to protect the extensive British interests in North Sea oil/gas installations and to patrol the 200 mile fishery limit. The future of the Class depends upon the outcome of a review into the future role and composition of the Fishery Protection Squadron- the requirement to patrol the North Sea Gas/Oil installations was withdrawn in 1993. JERSEY paid off for disposal in late 1993.

P A T R O L   V E S S E L S

HMS Peacock

PEACOCK CLASS

Ship	Pennant Number	Completion Date	Builder
PEACOCK	P239	1983	Hall Russell
PLOVER	P240	1983	Hall Russell
STARLING	P241	1984	Hall Russell

Displacement 700 tons **Dimensions** 60m x 10m x 5m **Speed** 28 knots **Armament** 1 - 76mm gun **Complement** 31.

Notes
The first warships to carry the 76mm Oto Melara gun. They are used to provide an ocean going back-up to the Marine Department of the Hong Kong Police. The Government of Hong Kong has paid 75% of the building and maintenance costs of these vessels. Sister ships SWALLOW and SWIFT returned to UK in 1988 and were sold (Oct 88) to the Irish Navy after only 3 years RN service. All three vessels are expected to remain in Hong Kong until 1997 and may then be sold to Eire.

HMS Pursuer

COASTAL TRAINING CRAFT ARCHER CLASS

Ship	Pennant Number	Completion Date	Builder
ARCHER	P264	1985	Watercraft
BITER	P270	1985	Watercraft
SMITER	P272	1986	Watercraft
PURSUER	P273	1988	Vosper
BLAZER	P279	1988	Vosper
DASHER	P280	1988	Vosper
PUNCHER	P291	1988	Vosper
CHARGER	P292	1988	Vosper
RANGER	P293	1988	Vosper
TRUMPETER	P294	1988	Vosper

Displacement 43 tonnes **Dimensions** 20m x 6m x 1m **Speed** 20 knots **Armament** Nil **Complement** 14.

Notes
In service with RN University units. TRUMPETER and RANGER deployed to Gibraltar in 1991.

33

HMS Cygnet

BIRD CLASS

Ship	Pennant Number	Completion Date	Builder
REDPOLE	P259	1970	Fairmile
KINGFISHER	P260	1975	R. Dunston
CYGNET	P261	1976	R. Dunston

Displacement 190 tons **Dimensions** 37m x 7m x 2m **Speed** 21 knots **Complement** 24.

Notes
REDPOLE commissioned into the Royal Navy in 1985 after service as an RAF search and rescue craft. All serve in the Northern Ireland Squadron and will be replaced by River Class vessels in due course.

● R.M. POOLE

HMS Messina

MESSINA CLASS

Ship	Pennant Number	Completion Date	Builder
MESSINA	A107	1982	R. Dunston

Displacement 127 tons **Dimensions** 25m x 6m x 2m **Speed** 10 knots **Complement** 9/13.

Notes
Very similar to the RMAS/RNXS tenders. MESSINA is a training ship for Royal Marines based at Poole,but will pay off during 1994. IXWORTH (A318), IRONBRIDGE (A311) are all former RMAS tenders now flying the White/Blue Ensign as diving tenders. DATCHET sold during 1993.

● D. HANNAFORD

HMS Roebuck

ROEBUCK CLASS

Ship	Pennant Number	Completion Date	Builder
ROEBUCK	A130	1986	Brooke Marine

Displacement 1500 tonnes **Dimensions** 64m x 13m x 4m **Speed** 15 knots **Complement** 47.

Notes
Was due to replace HECLA in the Survey fleet until the latter reprieved in 1987 for further service. Fitted with the latest fixing aids and sector scanning sonar.

HMS Hecla

HECLA CLASS

Ship	Pennant Number	Completion Date	Builder
HECLA	A133	1965	Yarrow
HERALD	A138	1974	Robb Caledon

Displacement 2,733 tons **Dimensions** 79m x 15m x 5m **Speed** 14 knots **Complement** 115.

Notes

Able to operate for long periods away from shore support, these ships and the smaller ships of the Hydrographic Fleet collect the data that is required to produce the Admiralty Charts and publications which are sold to mariners worldwide. HERALD is an improved version of the earlier ships. HECATE remains (late 1993) for sale at Portsmouth.

SURVEY SHIPS

HMS Beagle

BULLDOG CLASS

Ship	Pennant Number	Completion Date	Builder
BULLDOG	A317	1968	Brooke Marine
BEAGLE	A319	1968	Brooke Marine

Displacement 1,088 tons **Dimensions** 60m x 11m x 4m **Speed** 15 knots
Complement 39.

Notes

Designed to operate in coastal waters. Both have been extensively refitted to extend hull life. FOX was sold for commercial service in December 1988. FAWN sold for commercial service as M/V RED FULMAR. GLEANER (A86) is a small inshore survey craft based at Portsmouth.

38

HMY Britannia

ROYAL YACHT

Ship	Pennant Number	Completion Date	Builder
BRITANNIA	A00	1954	J. Brown

Displacement 5,280 tons **Dimensions** 126m x 17m x 5m **Speed** 21 knots **Complement** 250.

Notes
Probably the best known ship in the Royal Navy, BRITANNIA was designed to be converted to a hospital ship in time of war but this conversion was not made during the Falklands or Gulf crisis and the role has now been abandoned. The only seagoing ship in the RN commanded by an Admiral.

39

HMS Endurance

ICE PATROL SHIP

Ship	Pennant Number	Completion Date	Builder
ENDURANCE	A171	1990	Ulstein-Hatlo

Displacement 5,129 tons **Dimensions** 91m x 17.9m x 6.5m **Speed** 14.9 knots
Armament Small arms **Aircraft** 2 Lynx **Complement** 113.

Notes
Chartered for only 7 months in late 1991 to replace the older vessel of the same name. Originally M/V POLAR CIRCLE, renamed HMS POLAR CIRCLE (A176) and then purchased by MOD(N) and renamed again in October 1992 to current name.

THE ROYAL FLEET AUXILIARY

The Royal Fleet Auxiliary Service (RFA) is a civilian manned fleet owned and operated by the Ministry of Defence. Its main task is to supply warships of the Royal Navy at sea with fuel, food, stores and ammunition which they need to remain operational while away from base. With so few bases overseas which can be guaranteed in time of tension – let alone during any conflict – it has become vital, over the years, that everything from the smallest nut and bolt to a complete aero engine is taken on any naval deployment away from our coasts. The lack of that nut and bolt could well stop a ship in its tracks – literally. Increasingly, the service also provides aviation support for the Royal Navy – together with amphibious support and secure sea transport for army units and their equipment.

With a Navy rapidly shrinking in size – and with more reductions possible – it is inevitable that reductions in the size of the fleet are being investigated and implemented as vessels come to the end of their service life. In recent years older vessels have left the fleet without replacement . Support ships are, however, vital if British Forces are to have a role (and thus need support) at any distance from our shores.

With the continuing problems getting FORT VICTORIA into service it is difficult to see how any audit report cannot but be highly critical of the continuing requirement for such a large vessel (and her sister ship) being brought into service.Designed to support a Navy that was to have been far bigger than it is now ever likely to be, these vessels should have suffered the fate of the Upholder class submarines.- offered to any party who would take them off the books.At the very least these huge (virtually unarmed) ships should be completed and laid up if no overseas navy would take them on.Monies urgently needs to be spent building -or perhaps preferably chartering, smaller ,more useful,vessels for both the size and current operating pattern of the current,and proposed, RN fleet.

SHIPS OF THE ROYAL FLEET AUXILIARY
Pennant Numbers

Ship	Pennant Number	Ship	Pennant Number	Ship	Pennant Number
BRAMBLELEAF	A81	ARGUS	A135	FORT GEORGE	A388
BAYLEAF	A109	GREY ROVER	A269	RESOURCE	A480
ORANGELEAF	A110	GOLD ROVER	A271	SIR BEDIVERE	L3004
OAKLEAF	A111	BLACK ROVER	A273	SIR GALAHAD	L3005
OLWEN	A122	FORT GRANGE	A385	SIR GERAINT	L3027
OLNA	A123	FORT AUSTIN	A386	SIR PERCIVALE	L3036
DILIGENCE	A132	FORT VICTORIA	A387	SIR TRISTRAM	L3505

A number of merchant ships are on charter to various MOD departments. They include MAERSK GANNET, MAERSK ASCENCION, ST BRANDAN, INDOMITABLE & OIL MARINER in support of the Falkland Island commitment. NORTHELLA, PROUD SEAHORSE, and MARINE EXPLORER have hydrographic, training/trials roles in UK waters.

● OFFICIAL PHOTO

RFA Olwen

'OL' CLASS

Ship	Pennant Number	Completion Date	Builder
OLWEN	A122	1965	Hawthorn Leslie
OLNA	A123	1966	Hawthorn Leslie

Displacement 36,000 tons **Dimensions** 197m x 26m x 10m **Speed** 19 knots **Complement** 92.

Notes
These ships can operate up to 3 Sea King helicopters.-and are frequently used for Helicopter training when ARGUS is not available. Dry stores can be carried – and transferred at sea – as well as a wide range of fuel, aviation spirit and lubricants.OLMEDA (A124) placed on Disposal List (Sales) in early 1994 as an economy measure. Replacement by New Construction or Charter is now under consideration.

● OFFICIAL PHOTO

RFA Gold Rover

ROVER CLASS

Ship	Pennant Number	Completion Date	Builder
GREY ROVER	A269	1970	Swan Hunter
GOLD ROVER	A271	1974	Swan Hunter
BLACK ROVER	A273	1974	Swan Hunter

Displacement 11,522 tons **Dimensions** 141m x 19m x 7m **Speed** 18 knots
Armament 2 - 20mm guns **Complement** 49/54

Notes
Small Fleet Tankers designed to supply HM ships with fresh water, dry cargo and refrig-
erated provisions as well as a range of fuel and lubricants. Helicopter deck but no
hangar. BLUE ROVER sold to Portugal 1993.

RFA Oakleaf

LEAF CLASS

Ship	Pennant Number	Completion Date	Builder
BRAMBLELEAF	A81	1980	Cammell Laird
BAYLEAF	A109	1982	Cammell Laird
ORANGELEAF	A110	1982	Cammell Laird
OAKLEAF	A111	1981	Uddevalla V

Displacement 37,747 tons **Dimensions** 170m x 26m x 12m **Speed** 14.5 knots
Complement 60.

Notes

All are ex merchant ships & are.mainly employed on freighting duties BRAMBLELEAF
is owned by MOD (N), the remainder are on charter. OAKLEAF differs from the other
ships of the class which are all commercial Stat 32 tankers. At 49,310 tons she is the
largest vessel in RFA/RN service. APPLELEAF taken over by the Royal Australian Navy
(as HMAS Westralia) in late 1989 – on a 5 years charter – with an option to purchase..

RFA Fort Austin

FORT CLASS I

Ship	Pennant Number	Completion Date	Builder
FORT GRANGE	A385	1978	Scott Lithgow
FORT AUSTIN	A386	1979	Scott Lithgow

Displacement 23,384 tons **Dimensions** 183m x 24m x 9m **Speed** 20 knots **Complement** 201, (120 RFA, 36 RNSTS & 45 RN).

Notes
Full hangar and maintenance facilities are provided and up to four Sea King helicopters can be carried for both the transfer of stores and anti-submarine protection of a group of ships. Both ships can be armed with 4 - 20mm guns mounted on the Scot platforms. Both are fitted with 3" Chaff Systems.

STORE SHIPS

45

RFA Fort George

FORT CLASS II

Ship	Pennant Number	Completion Date	Builder
FORT VICTORIA	A387	1992	Harland & Wolff
FORT GEORGE	A388	1993	Swan Hunter

Displacement 31,500 tons **Dimensions** 204m x 30m x 9m **Speed** 20 knots
Armament 4 - 30mm guns, Sea Wolf Missile System (Fitted for but not with)
Complement 100 (RFA), 24 civilians, 32 RN and up to 122 aircrew.

Notes
 "One stop" replenishment ships with the widest range of armaments, fuel and spares
carried.Can operate up to 5 Sea King Helicopters with full maintenance facilities
onboard. Delays at the builder resulted in the plans for FORT VICTORIA to enter service in 1992 being abandoned.-She spent most of 1993 at Birkenhead & Portsmouth for
defect rectification.FORT GEORGE undergoing trials in 1993.

RFA Resource

REGENT CLASS

Ship	Pennant Number	Completion Date	Builder
RESOURCE	A480	1967	Scotts

Displacement 23,256 tons **Dimensions** 195m x 24m x 8m **Speed** 21 knots **Armament** 2 - 20mm guns **Complement** 160, (RFA 112, RNSTS 37, RN 11).

Notes
The widest range of naval armament stores are carried onboard plus a limited range of general naval stores and food. When the Wessex 5 was withdrawn from service in April 1987 the ship lost its permanently embarked helicopter but retains full flight deck facilities. RESOURCE reverted to Reserve (Preservation by Operation) status at Rosyth in November 1991 but brought forward in late 1992 for service in the Adriatic.She remained at Split throughout 1993. REGENT sold to India for scrap 1993.

47

• OFFICIAL PHOTO

RFA Sir Bedivere

LANDING SHIPS
SIR LANCELOT CLASS

Ship		Pennant Number	Completion Date	Builder
SIR BEDIVERE	•	L3004	1967	Hawthorn
SIR GALAHAD		L3005	1987	Swan Hunter
SIR GERAINT	•	L3027	1967	Stephen
SIR PERCIVALE	•	L3036	1968	Hawthorn
SIR TRISTRAM		L3505	1967	Hawthorn

Displacement 5,550 tons **Dimensions** 126m x 18m x 4m **Speed** 17 knots **Armament** Can be fitted with 20 or 40mm guns in emergency **Complement** 65, (SIR GALAHAD is larger at 8,451 tons. 140m x 20m **Complement** 58).

Notes

Manned by the RFA but tasked by the Army, these ships are used for heavy secure transport of stores – embarked by bow and stern doors – and beach assault landings. Can operate helicopters from both vehicle and flight deck if required-and carry 340 troops. SIR LANCELOT sold for commercial service in 1989.but by 1993 was in service with the Singapore Navy.
SIR TRISTRAM was rebuilt after extensive Falklands War damage. • Consideration is being given to rebuild/extend these vessels to prolong their service careers

48

HMS Ark Royal

RFA Oakleaf

HMS York

HMS Lancaster

F229

HMS Fearleass & RFA Sir Galahad

HMS Hurworth

l. to r.: HMS Monmouth, RFA
Fort George & HMS Norfolk

RFA Diligence

Ship	Pennant Number	Completion Date	Builder
DILIGENCE	A132	1981	Oesundsvarvet

Displacement 5,814 tons **Dimensions** 120m x 12m x 3m **Speed** 15 knots **Armament** 2 - 20mm **Complement** RFA 40. RN Personnel – approx 100.

Notes

Formerly the M/V Stena Inspector purchased (£25m) for service in the South Atlantic. Accommodation is provided for a 100 man Fleet Maintenance Unit. Her deep diving complex was removed and workshops added. Has given valuable support to a wide range of warships in the Falklands and Gulf.

RFA Argus

Ship	Pennant Number	Completion Date	Builder
ARGUS	A135	1981	Cantieri Navali Breda

Displacement 28,081 tons (full load) **Dimensions** 175m x 30m x 8m **Speed** 18 knots **Armament** 4 - 30mm, 2 - 20mm **Complement** 254 (inc 137 Air Group) **Aircraft** 6 Sea King, 12 Harriers can be carried in a "ferry role".

Notes

Formerly the M/V CONTENDER BEZANT taken up from trade during the Falklands crisis. Purchased in 1984 (£13 million) for conversion to an 'Aviation Training Ship'. A £50 million re-build was undertaken at Belfast from 1984-87. Undertook rapid conversion in October 1990 to "Primary Casualty Reception Ship" (Hospital Ship!) for service in the Gulf. These facilities remain "mothballed" on board for activation if required.

ROYAL MARITIME
AUXILIARY SERVICE

The RMAS Fleet is administered by the Director of Marine Services (Naval) to whom the Marine Services Managers at the various Naval Bases are mainly responsible for the provision of Marine Services to the RN / RFA Fleet - and other users in the MoD and other Government departments.(The position of Marine Services Manager was introduced during 1993 as Naval Officers, in positions such as Captains of the Ports ,were replaced by civilians.)

The Marine Services will become a Defence Agency on 1st April 1994 as part of the process of introducing market testing when,in 1996 the whole of the Marine Services organisation will offered out to competitive tender. The RMAS Fleet (of some 350 hulls) continues to be reduced in size as the size of the Royal Navy is itself reduced -and in preparation for market testing.The size of the Fleet is however still "customer driven" and vessels with low usage continue in service even though a reduced requirement for them may exist.In 1993 a consultants report on the service came up with some highly critical remarks regarding the Fleets effectiveness and manning levels when compared to commercial operators.

Ships of the RMAS, which can be seen at work in all the Naval Bases throughout the United Kingdom and at Gibraltar, are easily identified by their black hulls, buff coloured superstructure and funnels, and by the RMAS flag, which is a blue ensign defaced in the fly by a yellow anchor over two wavy lines. Pennant numbers are painted only on those vessels that are normally employed outside harbour limits.

● MARITIME PHOTOGRAPHIC

SHIPS OF
THE ROYAL MARITIME AUXILIARY SERVICE
Pennant Numbers

Ship	Pennant Number	Ship	Pennant Number
CAMERON	A72	KITTY	A170
MELTON	A83	LESLEY	A172
MENAI	A84	LILAH	A174
MEON	A87	MARY	A175
MILFORD	A91	EDITH	A177
FELICITY	A112	HUSKY	A178
MAGNET	A114	MASTIFF	A180
LODESTONE	A115	IRENE	A181
CAIRN	A126	SALUKI	A182
TORRENT	A127	ISABEL	A183
DALMATIAN	A129	SALMOOR	A185
TORNADO	A140	SALMASTER	A186
TORCH	A141	SALMAID	A187
TORMENTOR	A142	SETTER	A189
TOREADOR	A143	JOAN	A190
WATERMAN	A146	JOYCE	A193
FRANCES	A147	GWENDOLINE	A196
FIONA	A148	SEALYHAM	A197
FLORENCE	A149	HELEN	A198
GENEVIEVE	A150	MYRTLE	A199
GEORGINA	A152	SPANIEL	A201
EXAMPLE	A153	NANCY	A202
EXPLORER	A154	NORAH	A205
DEERHOUND	A155	LLANDOVERY	A207
DAPHNE	A156	LAMLASH	A208
LOYAL HELPER	A157	LECHLADE	A211
SUPPORTER	A158	BEE	A216
LOYAL WATCHER	A159	LOYAL MODERATOR	A220
LOYAL VOLUNTEER	A160	FORCEFUL	A221
LOYAL MEDIATOR	A161	NIMBLE	A222
ELKHOUND	A162	POWERFUL	A223
EXPRESS	A163	ADEPT	A224
GOOSANDER	A164	BUSTLER	A225
POCHARD	A165	CAPABLE	A226
KATHLEEN	A166	CAREFUL	A227
EXPLOIT	A167	FAITHFUL	A228
LABRADOR	A168	CRICKET	A229

Ship	Pennant Number	Ship	Pennant Number
COCKCHAFER	A230	CRICKLADE	A381
DEXTEROUS	A231	ARROCHAR	A382
ADAMANT	A232	APPLEBY	A383
GNAT	A239	CLOVELLY	A389
SHEEPDOG	A250	CRICCIETH	A391
LYDFORD	A251	GLENCOE	A392
LADYBIRD	A253	DUNSTER	A393
MEAVEY	A254	FINTRY	A394
CICALA	A263	GRASMERE	A402
SCARAB	A272	CROMARTY	A488
AURICULA	A285	DORNOCH	A490
ILCHESTER	A308	ROLLICKER	A502
INSTOW	A309	HEADCORN	A1766
FOXHOUND	A326	HEVER	A1767
BASSET	A327	HARLECH	A1768
COLLIE	A328	HAMBLEDON	A1769
CORGI	A330	LOYAL CHANCELLOR	A1770
IMPULSE	A344	LOYAL PROCTOR	A1771
IMPETUS	A345	HOLMWOOD	A1772
FELSTED	A348	HORNING	A1773
ELKSTONE	A353	WATERSPOUT	Y19
EPWORTH	A355	OILPRESS	Y21
ROYSTERER	A361	OILWELL	Y23
DENMEAD	A363	OILBIRD	Y25
FULBECK	A365	OILMAN	Y26
ROBUST	A366	WATERCOURSE	Y30
NEWTON	A367	WATERFOWL	Y31
WARDEN	A368	MOORHEN	Y32
KINTERBURY	A378	MOORFOWL	Y33

● I. BIGNELL

RMAS Roysterer

ROYSTERER CLASS

Ship	Pennant Number	Completion Date	Builder
ROYSTERER	A361	1972	C.D. Holmes
ROBUST	A366	1974	C.D. Holmes
ROLLICKER	A502	1973	C.D. Holmes

G.R.T. 1,036 tons **Dimensions** 54m x 12m x 6m **Speed** 15 knots **Complement** 21.

Notes

Built for salvage and long range towage, a role they only fulfil infrequently. They are, however, used for various "deepwater" trials for MOD research departments.Future employment unclear as economies are made throughout the service.

• H. BALLARD

RMAS Impulse

IMPULSE CLASS

Ship	Pennant Number	Completion Date	Builder
IMPULSE	A344	1993	Dunston
IMPETUS	A345	1993	Dunston

G.R.T. 400 tons approx **Dimensions** 33m x 10m x 4m **Speed** 12 knots **Complement** 5.

Notes

Two new tugs completed in 1993 to serve as berthing tugs for the Trident Class submarines at Faslane. It is hoped a smaller version will replace the Dog Class in due course.

RMAS Bustler

HARBOUR TUGS
TWIN UNIT TRACTOR TUGS (TUTT'S)

Ship	Pennant Number	Completion Date	Builder
FORCEFUL	A221	1985	R. Dunston
NIMBLE	A222	1985	R. Dunston
POWERFUL	A223	1985	R. Dunston
ADEPT	A224	1980	R. Dunston
BUSTLER	A225	1981	R. Dunston
CAPABLE	A226	1981	R. Dunston
CAREFUL	A227	1982	R. Dunston
FAITHFUL	A228	1985	R. Dunston
DEXTEROUS	A231	1986	R. Dunston

G.R.T. 375 tons **Dimensions** 39m x 10m x 4m **Speed** 12 knots **Complement** 9.

Notes
The principal harbour tug in naval service. CAPABLE is at Gibraltar.

RMAS Dalmatian

DOG CLASS

Ship	Pennant Number	Ship	Pennant Number
CAIRN •	A126	SETTER	A189
DALMATIAN	A129	SEALYHAM	A197
DEERHOUND	A155	SPANIEL	A201
ELKHOUND	A162	SHEEPDOG	A250
LABRADOR	A168	FOXHOUND	A326
HUSKY	A178	BASSET	A327
MASTIFF	A180	COLLIE •	A328
SALUKI	A182	CORGI	A330

G.R.T. 152 tons **Dimensions** 29m x 8m x 4m **Speed** 12 knots **Complement** 5.

Notes

General harbour tugs – all completed between 1962 and 1972.
• No longer tugs. Refitted as trials vessels for service at Kyle of Lochalsh.
ALSATIAN & POINTER sold in late 1993. CORGI in reserve at Devonport.
Replacements for this class are due - a smaller version of the IMPULSE class is proposed (with a 30 tonnes bollard pull) when/if funding is secured.

RMAS Daphne

IMPROVED GIRL CLASS

Ship	Pennant Number	Ship	Pennant Number
DAPHNE	A156	EDITH	A177

G.R.T. 75 tons **Speed** 10 knots **Complement** 4.

Notes
All completed 1971-2. DAISY, DORIS, CHARLOTTE and CHRISTINE sold 1989 and DOROTHY in 1990. Both vessels will run on until they are uneconomical to maintain. There are no plans to replace them.

RMAS Kitty

IRENE CLASS

Ship	Pennant Number	Ship	Pennant Number
KATHLEEN	A166	ISABEL	A183
KITTY	A170	JOAN	A190
LESLEY	A172	JOYCE	A193
LILAH	A174	MYRTLE	A199
MARY	A175	NANCY	A202
IRENE	A181	NORAH	A205

G.R.T. 89 tons **Speed** 8 knots **Complement** 4.

Notes
Known as Water Tractors these craft are used for basin moves and towage of light barges.

RMAS Felicity

FELICITY CLASS

Ship	Pennant Number	Ship	Pennant Number
FELICITY	A112	GENEVIEVE	A150
FRANCES	A147	GEORGINA	A152
FIONA	A148	GWENDOLINE	A196
FLORENCE	A149	HELEN	A198

G.R.T. 80 tons **Speed** 10 knots **Complement** 4.

Notes
Water Tractors – completed in 1973; FRANCES, FLORENCE and GENEVIEVE completed 1980.

68

● C. HOCKADAY

RMAS Newton

RESEARCH VESSEL

Ship	Pennant Number	Completion Date	Builder
NEWTON	A367	1976	Scotts

G.R.T. 2,779 tons **Dimensions** 99m x 16m x 6m **Speed** 15 knots **Complement** 39

Notes
An underwater research vessel with a limited cable laying capability.
The Trials ship RMAS WHITEHEAD was sold for scrap (in India) in 1993.

TRIALS SHIPS

RMAS Auricula

TEST & EXPERIMENTAL SONAR TENDER

Ship	Pennant Number	Completion Date	Builder
AURICULA	A285	1981	Ferguson Bros

G.R.T. 981 tons **Dimensions** 52m x 11m x 3m **Speed** 12 knots **Complement** 20.

Notes

Employed on evaluation work of new sonar equipment that may equip RN ships of the future. Based at Portland.Its future employment after 1996 when the Portland base closes is unclear.

RMAS Kinterbury

ARMAMENT STORES CARRIERS

Ship	Pennant Number	Completion Date	Builder
KINTERBURY	A378	1980	Appledore SB
ARROCHAR	A382	1981	Appledore SB

G.R.T. 1,357 tons **Dimensions** 64m x 12m x 5m **Speed** 14 knots **Complement** 19.

Notes
2 holds carry Naval armament stores, ammunition and guided missiles. Both vessels vary slightly. ARROCHAR (ex ST GEORGE) taken over in late 1988 from the Army. Both vessels have enough employment within the RMAS for the foreseeable future.

RMAS Bee

INSECT CLASS

Ship	Pennant Number	Completion Date	Builder
BEE	A216	1970	C.D. Holmes
CRICKET *	A229	1972	Beverley
COCKCHAFER	A230	1971	Beverley
GNAT	A239	1972	Beverley
LADYBIRD	A253	1973	Beverley
CICALA *	A263	1971	Beverley
SCARAB	A272	1973	Beverley

G.R.T. 279 tons **Dimensions** 34m x 8m x 3m **Speed** 10.5 knots **Complement** 7-9.

Notes
CRICKET and SCARAB are fitted as Mooring Vessels and COCKCHAFER as a Trials Stores Carrier – remainder are Naval Armament carriers.* For Disposal 1994.

XSV Loyal Moderator

LOYAL CLASS

Ship	Pennant Number	Ship	Pennant Number
XSV LOYAL HELPER	A157	XSV LOYAL MEDIATOR	A161
XSV SUPPORTER	A158	XSV LOYAL MODERATOR	A220
XSV LOYAL WATCHER	A159	XSV LOYAL CHANCELLOR	A1770
XSV LOYAL VOLUNTEER	A160	XSV LOYAL PROCTOR	A1771

G.R.T. 112 tons **Dimensions** 24m x 6m x 3m **Speed** 10.5 knots **Complement** 24.

Notes
All these craft have been operated by the Royal Naval Auxiliary Service (RNXS) who, in time of emergency, would man them as port control vessels. It was decided however in 1993 that this role was no longer needed and the service will be disbanded by 31st March 1994. LOYAL CHANCELLOR & LOYAL WATCHER will transfer to RN University units - the remainder being placed on the disposal list.

TENDERS

RMAS Adamant

ADAMANT

Ship	Pennant Number	Completion Date	Builder
ADAMANT	A232	1992	FBM (Cowes)

GRT 170 tonnes **Dimensions** 30m x 8m x 1m **Speed** 22 knots **Complement** 5

Notes
Twin catamaran hulls based on the commercial Red Jet design (as used by Red Funnel Ferry Co). First water jet propulsion vessel in the RMAS. In service as a Clyde personnel ferry.

RMAS Lamlash

(TYPE A, B & X) TENDERS

Ship	Pennant Number	Ship	Pennant Number
MELTON	A83	CRICKLADE	A381
MENAI	A84	CLOVELLY	A389
MEON	A87	CRICCIETH	A391
MILFORD	A91	GLENCOE	A392
LLANDOVERY	A207	LAMLASH	A208
FINTRY	A394	GRASMERE	A402
LECHLADE	A211	CROMARTY	A488
LYDFORD	A251	DORNOCH •	A490
ILCHESTER •	A308	HEADCORN	A1766
INSTOW •	A309	HEVER	A1767
FELSTED	A348	HARLECH	A1768
ELKSTONE	A353	HAMBLEDON	A1769
EPWORTH	A355	HOLMWOOD	A1772
FULBECK	A365	HORNING	A1773

G.R.T. 78 tons **Dimensions** 24m x 6m x 3m **Speed** 10.5 knots **Complement** 4/5.

Notes

All completed since 1971 to replace Motor Fishing Vessels. Vessels marked • are diving tenders. Remainder are Training Tenders, Passenger Ferries, or Cargo Vessels. GLENCOE (ex RMAS) now with RNR at Southampton. DENMEAD with RNR at Belfast. MEAVEY operates for HMS SULTAN as SULTAN VENTURER •,DUNSTER for disposal.

75

XSV Express

COASTAL TRAINING CRAFT
EXAMPLE CLASS

Ship	Pennant Number	Completion Date	Builder
XSV EXAMPLE	A153	1985	Watercraft
XSV EXPLORER	A154	1985	Watercraft
XSV EXPRESS	A163	1988	Vosper T
XSV EXPLOIT	A167	1988	Vosper T

Displacement 43 tons **Dimensions** 20m x 6m x 1m **Speed** 20 knots **Armament** Nil
Complement 14

Notes
Training vessels for the RNXS-until the organisation is disbanded by 31March
1994.Vessels will then be transferred to RN University Units as sea training tenders.

RMAS Oilwell

COASTAL OILERS
OILPRESS CLASS

Ship	Pennant Number	Completion Date	Builder
OILPRESS	Y21	1969	Appledore Shipbuilders
OILWELL	Y23	1969	Appledore Shipbuilders
OILBIRD	Y25	1969	Appledore Shipbuilders
OILMAN	Y26	1969	Appledore Shipbuilders

G.R.T. 362 tons **Dimensions** 41m x 9m x 3m **Speed** 11 knots **Complement** 5.

Notes
Employed as Harbour and Coastal Oilers. OILSTONE sold 17 Dec 92.

RMAS Watercourse

WATER CARRIERS
WATER CLASS

Ship	Pennant Number	Completion Date	Builder
WATERSPOUT	Y19	1967	Drypool Eng Co
WATERCOURSE	Y30	1974	Drypool Eng Co
WATERFOWL	Y31	1974	Drypool Eng Co
WATERMAN	A146	1978	R. Dunston

G.R.T. 263 tons **Dimensions** 40m x 8m x 2m **Speed** 11 knots **Complement** 5.

Notes

Capable of coastal passages, these craft normally supply either demineralised or fresh water to the Fleet within port limits. WATERSHED sold to Malta October 1992.

RMAS Lodestone

DEGAUSSING VESSELS
MAGNET CLASS

Ship	Pennant Number	Completion Date	Builder
MAGNET	A114	1979	Cleland
LODESTONE	A115	1980	Cleland

G.R.T. 828 tons **Dimensions** 55m x 12m x 4m **Speed** 14 knots **Complement** 9.

Notes
LODESTONE is operational (on the Clyde). MAGNET in reserve (Portsmouth).

• C. HOCKADAY

RMAS Torrent

TORPEDO RECOVERY VESSELS (TRV'S)
TORRID CLASS

Ship	Pennant Number	Completion Date	Builder
TORRENT	A127	1971	Cleland SB Co

G.R.T. 550 tons **Dimensions** 46m x 9m x 3m **Speed** 12 knots **Complement** 14.

Notes
A stern ramp is built for the recovery of torpedoes fired for trials and exercises. A total of 32 can be carried. In Reserve.

RMAS Toreador

TORNADO CLASS

Ship	Pennant Number	Completion Date	Builder
TORNADO	A140	1979	Hall Russell
TORCH	A141	1980	Hall Russell
TORMENTOR	A142	1980	Hall Russell
TOREADOR	A143	1980	Hall Russell

G.R.T. 560 tons **Dimensions** 47m x 8m x 3m **Speed** 14 knots **Complement** 13.

Notes
TORMENTOR is based at Plymouth – remainder on the Clyde. All vessels have had suitable rails fitted to enable them to operate as exercise minelayers.TOREADOR is in reserve on the Clyde.

T
R
V'
s

RMAS Salmoor

MOORING & SALVAGE VESSELS
SAL CLASS

Ship	Pennant Number	Completion Date	Builder
SALMOOR	A185	1985	Hall Russell
SALMASTER	A186	1986	Hall Russell
SALMAID	A187	1986	Hall Russell

Displacement 2200 tonnes **Dimensions** 77m x 15m x 4m **Speed** 15 knots **Complement** 17.

Notes
Multi-purpose vessels designed to lay and maintain underwater targets and moorings and undertake a wide range of salvage tasks.

RMAS Goosander

WILD DUCK CLASS

Ship	Pennant Number	Completion Date	Builder
GOOSANDER	A164	1973	Robb Caledon

G.R.T. 900 tons* **Dimensions** 58mm x 12m x 4m **Speed** 10 knots **Complement** 18.

Notes

Capable of carrying out a wide range of duties laying moorings and heavy lift salvage work. 200 tons can be lifted over the bow. POCHARD is in reserve at Portsmouth but unlikely to see further service as she is being used as a source of spares to keep GOOSANDER operational.Due to be replaced on the Clyde in April 1995 by SALMAID.

M
S
V's
S

RMAS Moorhen

MOOR CLASS

Ship	Pennant Number	Completion Date	Builder
MOORHEN	Y32	1989	McTay Marine
MOORFOWL	Y33	1989	McTay Marine
CAMERON	A72	1991	Richard Dunston

Displacement 518 tons **Dimensions** 32m x 11m x 2m **Speed** 8 knots **Complement** 10

Notes

Powered mooring lighters for use within sheltered coastal waters. (MOORHEN at Portsmouth, MOORFOWL at Devonport). CAMERON is similar but is employed as an Underwater Trials & Experimental vessel at Rosyth.

RMAS Warden

WARDEN CLASS

Ship	Pennant Number	Completion Date	Builder
WARDEN	A368	1989	Richards

Displacement 626 tons **Dimensions** 48m x 10m x 4m **Speed** 15 knots **Complement** 11.

Notes
Range Mooring Vessel for RAE Aberporth (S. Wales). Based at Pembroke Dock. Fitted with 30 tonne bollard pull towing winch to provide alternative employment for her.

The Director of Marine Services (Naval) is also responsible for the contract management of the RAF and Army Range Safety Groups. The operation of both these organisations was re- offered for tender in 1993, with A V Seawork being the successful tenderer. The contracts normally run for three years when they are again offered for competitive tender.

Details of Army Range Safety Craft are as follows:

Ship	Pennant Number	Completion Date	Builder
FALCONET	Y01	1983	James & Stone
PETARD	Y02	1983	James & Stone

G.R.T. 70 tons **Dimensions** 24m x 5.5m x 2.5m **Speed** 21 knots **Complement** 5.

There are also eleven smaller range safety craft; details below:

G.R.T. 19.68 tonnes **Dimensions** 14.9m x 4.66m x 1.67. **Speed** 22 knots **Complement** 3.

Their primary tasks are range surveillance and clearance, target towing for weapon attacks and the recovery of Sonobuoys, maritime weapons and training devices in coastal range areas. The craft are based at Pembroke Dock, Weymouth, Dover, Whitehaven and Loch Boisdale.

Details of RAF Range Craft are as follows:

LRRSC (Long Range Recovery and Support Craft)

Ship	Pennant Number	Completion Date	Builder
SEAL	5000	1967	Brooke Marine
SEAGULL	5001	1970	Fairmile Const.

G.R.T. 159 tons **Dimensions** 120' 3" x 23' 6" x 5' 11" **Speed** 21 knots **Complement** 6.

RTTL (Rescue, Target Towing Launches)

SPITFIRE, HALIFAX, HAMPDEN, HURRICANE, LANCASTER & WELLINGTON

G.R.T. 71 tons **Dimensions** 22m x 5.6m x 1.6m **Speed** 21 knots

There are also 3 x 63' Pinnaces Nos 1374, 1389 & 1392.

These craft are employed on target towing, SAR, various trials and weapon recovery. They are based at Invergordon, Great Yarmouth and Holyhead.

• C. HOCKADAY

HMAV Ardennes

ARMY LANDING CRAFT
LCL CLASS (LANDING CRAFT LOGISTIC)

Vessel	Pennant Number	Completion Date	Builder
HMAV Ardennes	L4001	1977	Brooke Marine
HMAV Arakan	L4003	1978	Brooke Marine

Displacement 1,050 tons **Dimensions** 72m x 15m x 2m **Speed** 10 knots **Complement** 36.

Notes
Designed to carry up to 520 tonnes of cargo, overside loaded, or up to Five Chieftain tanks – Ro Ro loaded, reducing to 254 tonnes for beaching operations, through bow doors. Principal roles are maintenance of the Royal Artillery Range Outer Hebrides and in support of Amphibious Operations and Exercises.

RCTV Audemer

RCL CLASS
(RAMPED CRAFT LOGISTIC)

Vessel	Pennant Number	Completion Date	Builder
RCTV Arromanches	L105	1981	Brooke Marine
RCTV Antwerp	L106	1981	Brooke Marine
RCTV Andalsnes	L107	1984	James & Stone
RCTV Abbeville	L108	1984	James & Stone
RCTV Akyab	L109	1984	James & Stone
RCTV Aachen	L110	1986	James & Stone
RCTV Arezzo	L111	1986	James & Stone
RCTV Agheila	L112	1987	James & Stone
RCTV Audemer	L113	1987	James & Stone

Displacement 165 tons **Dimensions** 33m x 8m x 1.5m **Speed** 9 knots **Complement** 6.

Notes
Smaller – "all purpose" landing craft capable of carrying up to 100 tons. In service in coastal waters around Cyprus, Hong Kong & UK.

Appleby

SEA CADET VESSELS

FLEET TENDERS 63 DESIGN

Ship	Pennant Number	Ship	Pennant Number
ABERDOVEY	Y10	ALNMOUTH	Y13
ABINGER	Y11	APPLEBY	A383

Displacement 117 tons **Dimensions** 24m x 5m x 3m **Speed** 10.5 knots.

Notes
'Craft are allocated to the Sea Cadet Corps. ABERDOVEY, Southern Area, Portsmouth based; ABINGER,Northern Area, Greenock based; ALNMOUTH, North West Area, Liverpool based; APPLEBY, South West Area, based at Portland (summer) and Bristol (winter).All vessels laid up during 1993 pending a decision to bring them up to current DTI standards.Work placed in hand (at Portland) and the vessels are expected to return to service in 1994

 Ex-BIBURY (A103) operates for Portsmouth Naval Base Sub Aqua Club.

British Aerospace Sea Harrier

Variants: FRS 1 FRS 2

Role: Short take off, vertical landing (STOVL) fighter and reconnaissance aircraft.

Engine: 1 x 21,500lb thrust Rolls Royce PEGASUS 104, turbojet.

Span 25' 3" **Length** 47' 7"(FRS2 49'1") **Height** 12' 0" **Max weight** 26,200lb.

Max speed Mach 1.2 **Crew** 1 pilot.

Avionics: FRS 1- Blue Fox pulse radar. FRS2 -Blue Vixen pulse doppler radar

Armament: FRS2 up to 4 x AMRAAM Air to Air Missiles.Both variants SEA EAGLE air to surface missiles. SIDEWINDER air to air missiles. 2 - 30mm Aden cannons with 120 rounds per gun in detachable pods, one either side of the lower fuselage. 1 fuselage centreline and 4 underwing hardpoints. The inner wing stations are capable of carrying 2,000lb of stores and are plumbed for drop tanks. The other positions can carry stores up to 1,000lb in weight. Possible loads include 1,000lb or practice bombs; BL 755 cluster bombs, Lepus flares, 190 or 100 gallon drop tanks. A single F95 camera is mounted obliquely in the nose for the reconnaissance role.

Squadron Service: 800, 801 and 899 squadrons in commission.

Notes: During 1994, 800 squadron will be embarked in HMS INVINCIBLE and 801 in HMS ARK ROYAL.(To ILLUSTRIOUS in late 1994) 899 squadron is responsible for the training of pilots and the development of tactics.It is normally shore based at Yeovilton. In a period of tension it could embark to reinforce the embarked air groups in the carriers.

• MARITIME PHOTOGRAPHIC

Westland SEA KING

Developed for the Royal Navy from the Sikorsky SH3D, the basic Sea King airframe is used in three different roles. The following details are common to all:
Engines: 2 x 1600shp Rolls Royce Gnome H 1400 – 1 free power turbines.
Rotor Diameter 62' 0" **Length** 54' 9" **Height** 17' 2" **Max Weight** 21,400lb **Max Speed** 125 knots.
The 3 versions are:-

● MARITIME PHOTOGRAPHIC

HAR 5 : HAS 6

The HAS6 has improved sonics, deeper dipping active sonar and ESM
Roles: Anti-submarine search and strike. SAR. Transport.
Crew: 2 pilots, 1 observer and 1 aircrewman.
Avionics: Sea Searcher radar; Type 195 variable depth active/passive sonar.LAPADS passive sonobuoy analyser. Orange Crop passive ESM equipment.
Armament: 4 fuselage hardpoints capable of carrying STINGRAY torpedoes or depth charges. Various flares, markers, grenades and sonobuoys can be carried internally and hand launched. A 7.62mm machine gun can be mounted in the doorway.
Squadron Service: 771 Squadron operates the HAR 5.706 810, 814, 819, and 820 squadrons are in commission equipped with HAS 6.
Notes: The Sea King has been the backbone of the Fleet Air Arm's anti-submarine force since 1970. 706 is the advanced training squadron at Culdrose. 810 is an operational training squadron with the capability to embark to reinforce the front line. During 1994, 814 squadron will be embarked in HMS INVINCIBLE and 820 in HMS ARK ROYAL.(to ILLUSTRIOUS in late 1994) 819 is shore based at Prestwick The HAR 5 has an excellent SAR capability which is frequently demonstrated in the south west approaches. The HAS 6 has less complete SAR facilities when full ASW equipment fitted.

AEW 2

Role: Airborne Early Warning. **Crew:** 1 pilot and 2 observers.
Avionics: Thorn/EMI Searchwater radar Orange Crop passive ESM equipment.
Squadron Service: 849 HQ, 849A and 849B flights in commission.
Notes: Used to detect low flying aircraft trying to attack aircraft carrier battle groups under conventional shipborne radar cover. Can also be used for surface search utilising its sophisticated, computerised long range radar. During 1994 849A flight will be embarked in HMS INVINCIBLE and 849B in HMS ARK ROYAL.(Will probably move to ILLUSTRIOUS in late 1994) 849HQ acts as a training and trials unit at Culdrose.

HC 4

Role: Commando assault and utility transport.
Crew: 1 pilot and 1 aircrewman.
Armament: Door mounted 7.62mm machine gun.
Squadron Service: 707, 772, 845 and 846 squadrons in commission.
Notes: The HC4 has a fixed undercarriage with no sponsons or radome.Can carrying up to 27 troops in the cabin or underslung loads up to 8,000lb in weight. 707 squadron is a training unit at Yeovilton. 845 & 846 squadrons are based at Yeovilton but embark or detach at short notice to support 3 Cdo Brigade.845 Sqdn has spent long periods in Split in support of UN Forces in Bosnia during 1993. 772 sqdn at Portland

Westland LYNX

Variants: HAS 3, HAS 3S, HAS 3CTS.

Roles: Surface search and strike; anti-submarine strike; SAR.

Engines: 2 x 900hp Rolls Royce GEM BS 360-07-26 free shaft turbines.

Rotor diameter: 42'0" **Length** 39' 1" **Height** 11' 0" **Max Weight** 9,500lb.

Max Speed: 150 knots. **Crew:** 1 pilot and 1 observer.

Avionics:i SEA SPRAY radar. I Orange Crop passive ESM equipment.

Armament: External pylons carry up to 4 - SEA SKUA air to surface missiles or 2-x STINGRAY, Mk 46 torpedoes, depth charges, flares or markers.

Squadron Service: 702, & 815 squadrons in commission.

Notes: 815 OEU FLT is a trials squadron with equipment for HAS 8 and 702 is a training squadron based at Portland. 815 squadron also based at Portland is the parent unit for single aircraft ships flights.Two versions of the Lynx, the AH1 & AH7are operated by the Royal Marines Brigade Air Squadron which is based at Yeovilton.

(HAS Mk 8) is now flying and undergoing intensive development trials.

The HAS 3S represents the first phase of developments that will lead to the HAS 8.The HAS 3CTS represents the second phase.Full HAS 8 aircraft are expected to be delivered in the mid 90's.

Westland GAZELLE HT2

Engine: 1 x 592shp Turbomeca ASTAZOU free power turbine.

Crew: 1 or 2 pilots.

Notes: In service with 705 squadron at Culdrose. Used for training all RN helicopter pilots up to "wings standard" before they move onto the Sea King or Lynx. A version of the Gazelle, the AH1, is used by the Royal Marines Brigade Air Squadron based at Yeovilton.

OTHER AIRCRAFT TYPES IN ROYAL NAVY SERVICE DURING 1994

British Aerospace JETSTREAM T2 and T3

Engines: 2 x 940hp Turbomeca ASTAZOU 16D turboprops. (T3 Garrett turboprops).
Crew: 1 or 2 pilots, 2 student observers plus 3 other seats.
Notes: T2's are used by 750 squadron at Culdrose for training Fleet Air Arm Observers. T3's are used by the Heron flight at Yeovilton.

de Havilland CHIPMUNK

Engine: 1 x 145hp de Havilland Gipsy Major 8 piston engine.
Crew: 2 pilots.
Notes: Used by the RN Flying Grading Flight at Roborough airport near Plymouth (and as such the first aircraft flown by generations of naval aircrew)

Hawker HUNTER T8, GA11, T7 & T8M

Engine: 1 x 7575lb thrust Rolls Royce AVON turbojet.
Crew: T8 1 or 2 pilots. GA11 1 pilot. T7 1 or 2 pilots. T8m 1 or 2 pilots.
Notes: The Royal Navy has used Hunters to train fixed wing pilots since 1958. A number remain in service at RNAS YEOVILTON with the RN flying standards flight and with FRADU who use them as airborne targets for the aircraft direction school. 899 Squadron also use these aircraft as radar trainers for Sea Harrier pilots.

In addition to these aircraft, the following aircraft have naval functions:
CANBERRA T17: Used by 360 joint RN/RAF Squadron for electronic warfare tasks. Based at RAF WYTON,but expected to be disbanded during 1994.
British Aerospace 125: Two aircraft, owned by the RN are operated by RN aircrew as part of 32 Squadron RAF based at RAF NORTHOLT- their future is unclear.

The Fleet Air Arm Historic flight based at Yeovilton has two **SWORDFISH, & a FIREFLY** on strength.These are often seen at air displays in the summer months. .

Full details of these and many other naval aircraft can be found in the revised edition of AIRCRAFT OF THE ROYAL NAVY SINCE 1945 published by Maritime Books.

At the end of the line ...

Readers may well find other warships afloat which are not mentioned in this book. The majority have fulfilled a long and useful life and are now relegated to non-seagoing duties. The following list gives details of their current duties:

Pennant Number	Ship	Remarks
A134	RAME HEAD	Escort Maintenance Vessel – Royal Marines Training Ship at Portland
C35	BELFAST	World War II Cruiser Museum ship – Pool of London Open to the public daily Tel: 071-407 6434
D23	BRISTOL	Type 82 Destroyer – Sea Cadet Training Ship at Portsmouth.
D73	CAVALIER	World War II Destroyer Museum Ship at Hebburn Not open to public. Future under consideration.
F126	PLYMOUTH	Type 12 Frigate & Oberon class Submarine Museum Ships at Birkenhead
S21	ONYX	Open to the public daily. Tel: 051 650 1573
M1115	BRONINGTON	Ton Class Minesweeper at Manchester Limited Opening to the Public Tel 061 877 7778
S67	ALLIANCE	Submarine – Museum Ship at Gosport Open to the public daily. Tel: 0705- 511485

At the time of publishing the following ships were awaiting tow for scrap or sale.

PORTSMOUTH

Jupiter	Juno
Sirius	Argonaut
Hecate	Oracle
Hermione	Opossum
Opportune	Scylla
Sheraton	Brinton
Nurton	Jersey

ROSYTH

Churchill
Dreadnought
Revenge
Swiftsure

PLYMOUTH

Conqueror
Courageous
Warspite